100 Years of
Crime
Twentieth Century in Pictures

D1157500

100 Years of
Crime
Twentieth Century in Pictures

AMMONITE
PRESS

**PRESS
ASSOCIATION**
Images

First Published 2009 by
Ammonite Press
an imprint of AE Publications Ltd,
166 High Street, Lewes, East Sussex BN7 1XU

Text copyright Ammonite Press
Images copyright Press Association Images
Copyright in the work Ammonite Press

ISBN 978-1-906672-29-4

British Cataloguing in Publication Data. A catalogue
record of this book is available from the British Library.

Editor: Daniel Neilson
Series Editor: Paul Richardson
Picture research: Press Association Images
Design: Gravemaker + Scott

Colour reproduction by GMC Reprographics
Printed by Kyodo Nation Printing Services

Page 2: The Home Secretary, Winston Churchill (L, in top hat), during the Siege of Sidney Street. He authorised the use of the Regiment of Scots Guards and artillery to flush out the anarchists.
3rd January, 1911

Page 5: Under the guidance of police officers, three hooded men are taken to waiting police cars at Linslade, Buckinghamshire, after being remanded in custody on charges in connection with the Great Train Robbery.
16th August, 1963

Page 6: A protester kicks the window of a fast food store in Lower Regent Street during rioting in London amid protests against the Conservative government's highly unpopular Community Charge, also known as the poll tax.
31st March, 1990

Introduction

Crime is an uneasy passion for those who commit it, those who fight it, those who judge it – and for the public who observe it. From the dockers' strike of 1911 to the poll tax riots in 1990, there is no clearer gauge of public opinion than an angry population taking to the streets. Some crimes enter the public consciousness in remarkable ways: those archetypal gangsters, the Kray Twins, rose to the status, almost, of folk heroes during the 1950s despite their brutal methods, as did the Great Train Robbers a decade later.

Violence, deception and death have long stirred the imagination of the British people despite the nation's apparent respectability. There are infamous cases from the early 20th century that could have been taken from a detective novel, and indeed *Sherlock Holmes* author Sir Arthur Conan-Doyle was called in on more than one real-life investigation. Notorious murders were given vivid titles by an excited media: the 'Acid Bath Murders' and 'Braybrook Street Massacre' were closely followed by a fascinated public, as were the proceedings against Crippen, Brady and 'Yorkshire Ripper' Sutcliffe. Trials attracted huge crowds outside courthouses during proceedings – and at the gates of prisons when murderers were executed.

No matter how many cases are closed, crime never escapes the flash of the photographer's bulb. From the Press Association's archive of more than 15 million pictures, wife-murderers, protesters, bank robbers, rioters and gunmen look out at us through the lenses of generations of determined news photographers. We see the imprisoned Suffragette Emmeline Pankhurst, legendary figures such as Lord Lucan, the aftermath of IRA bomb attacks in London and the inner city riots of the 1980s. No written description could carry so much power, could transport us to the events portrayed, so effectively.

Along with law-breaking goes crime-fighting: the story of the British police, on foot and horse a hundred years ago and in cars and helicopters today, can be read in these pictures. Politicians too: thus we see a young Winston Churchill at the Sydney Street Siege of 1911 and PC George Scorey with his grey horse Billy quelling a Wembley crowd in 1923: would a Home Secretary place himself in the line of fire, would a horse emerge as a hero of law enforcement, today?

Perhaps. But the most compelling questions raised by this collection of images come when looking directly into the eyes of a killer.

One of the founders of the British Suffragette movement, Emmeline Pankhurst (R) is seen in prison costume along with her daughter Christabel. Emmeline Pankhurst described her first spell in jail as: *"a human being in the process of being turned into a wild beast"*.

1st June, 1908

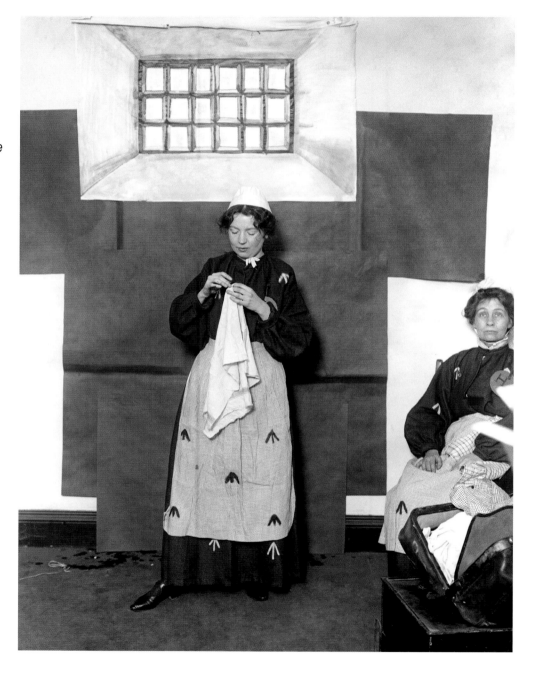

Chief Inspector Scott (R), Superintendent Taylor (C), and
Detective Inspector Fowle (L), investigate the murder of
Caroline Luard, the wife of Major-General Charles Luard. Her
body was found on the 24th of August 1908, near their home
in Ightham, Kent, with two bullet wounds to her head and her
purse and rings missing. The case became known as the
Seal Chart Murder after the summerhouse where she died.
26th August, 1908

The coroner at the inquest of the murder of Caroline Luard.
Some blamed her husband Charles Luard for murdering
her to cover up an affair, but the inquest found "*a person or
persons unknown*" killed her.
27th August, 1908

Major-General Charles
Luard at the funeral of
his wife, Caroline Luard,
after the so-called Seal
Chart Murder.
28th August, 1908

Captain Charles Luard (L) on his way to the inquest of his father Major-General Charles Luard who jumped in front of the 9.09 train from Maidstone to Tonbridge on the 17th of September 1908. In a letter to his son he blamed his suicide on the "*horrid letters and insinuations that have been made*" in reference to the murder of his wife.

19th September, 1908

Suffragette Emmeline Pethick-Lawrence on her release
from Holloway Prison. She had joined Emmeline Pankurst's
Women's Social and Political Union that used increasingly
disruptive methods to secure votes for women.
17th April, 1909

George Joseph Smith (alias Henry Williams) and his new wife Beatrice 'Bessie' Munday. She was the first of three victims Smith murdered in their baths along with Alice Burnham and Margaret Elizabeth Lofty. He was executed at Maidstone Gaol, Kent, on the 13th of August 1915, for what became known as the 'Brides in the Bath' murders. He would have financially benefited from their deaths.
1st June, 1910

Dr Hawley Harvey Crippen (third R) and his lover Ethel Le Neve (second R), poorly disguised as his son, leaving the liner *SS Montrose* escorted by Inspector Walter Dew. They were arrested in Quebec, Canada, after being pursued across the Atlantic in a chase that gripped the nation.

6th August, 1910

Facing page: A crowd surges forward to get a glimpse of the American physician Dr Hawley Harvey Crippen and his lover Ethel Le Neve as they arrive, under arrest, at Liverpool for murdering Crippen's estranged wife Cora Turner.

6th August, 1910

Dr Hawley Harvey Crippen with Ethel Le Neve, during their trial for the murder of his wife Cora Turner. It emerged he burned her bones on the kitchen stove, dissolved her organs in acid and disposed of her head in the English Channel on a day trip to France. He was found guilty and hanged at Pentonville Prison on the 23rd of November 1910. Ethel Le Neve was acquitted.

30th September, 1910

Facing page: Guardsmen take aim during the siege at 100 Sidney Street, east London, where soldiers from the Tower of London and police fought a gun battle with three Latvian 'anarchists'. The previous day, the gang had killed three officers in a botched raid on a nearby jewellery shop and had taken shelter at this house.

3rd January, 1911

Police frog-marching a prisoner in Liverpool.
1911

The burning house where the anarchists were holed up during the Sidney Street siege. The scorched bodies of two people were found, but the leader, known as 'Peter the Painter', was never discovered.

3rd January, 1911

Soldiers in firing position
during the Sidney Street
siege.
3rd January, 1911

Stinie Morrison in the dock at the Old Bailey during his trial for the murder of Leon Beron. Morrison murdered Leon Beron, a Russian Jewish emigrant and a slum landlord, on the 1st of January 1911. The letter 'S' was carved into his cheek; it represents 'spy' in Russian and Polish. Morrison's sentence was death, but Home Secretary Winston Churchill commuted it to life.

6th March, 1911

Protesters arrested after assaulting a police officer during the Liverpool railway and dock strike of 1911. The 72-day walk out, sparked by complaints about seamen's poor wages, became one of the bitterest industrial disputes of the time and spread around the country.

13th August, 1911

Sir Edward Henry, Commissioner of the Police of the Metropolis. On the 27th of November 1911 he was shot by a cab driver whose licence application had been refused. Despite being hit in the abdomen, he survived and the would-be killer was shot by Sir Edward's chauffeur.
1911

The City of London
Mounted Police.
1911

The mother, sister and brother of Hugh Trevanion who committed suicide after his lover, Albert Roe, left him. He had attempted to commit suicide three times previously to stop Roe marrying a girl.
20th January, 1913

Albert Roe (L) arriving with some friends at Hove Town Hall for the inquiry into the suicide of his former lover Hugh Trevanion. Trevanion's estranged family demanded the inquiry after they were cut out of the wealthy young man's will in favour of Roe.

20th January, 1913

Sir Charles Matthews (L), the Director of Public Prosecutions and the well-known barrister Richard Muir (R) arriving at Hove Town Hall for the inquiry into the suicide of Hugh Trevanion. The inquest returned an open verdict and Roe was allowed the full inheritance. Had the verdict been different, Roe could have been charged with murder as demanded by the enraged relatives.

20th January, 1913

Facing page: St Catherine's Church, Hatcham, in flames after an arson attack by a militant arm of the Suffragette movement. The church was targeted for condemning the Suffragettes.

14th May, 1913

A policeman restrains
a Suffragette outside
Buckingham Palace where
a group were trying to
deliver a petition to the King.
21st May, 1914

Facing page: A Suffragette
being arrested by police
officers.
1914

Facing page: Suffragette Mary Spencer in the dock charged with causing criminal damage to the nude painting *Primavera* by Sir George Clausen in London's National Gallery. She was jailed in Holloway but later released under a government amnesty after the outbreak of the First World War.

23rd May, 1914

Alfred Arthur Rouse (aged 20) on the day he enlisted with the 24th Queen's Territorial Regiment as a Private. In 1930 Rouse, shell-shocked after a bomb exploded in his trench, attempted to fabricate his own death by picking up a hitchhiker, knocking him out and then burning his car with the man inside. The identity of the deceased was never discovered.

8th August, 1914

George Joseph Smith, convicted of murdering Beatrice Mundy, Alice Burnham and Margaret Elizabeth Lofty in the notorious 'Brides In The Bath' case. It is still one of the most famous investigations conducted by the London Metropolitan Police.

1st August, 1915

DIE KARTE MIT DER LETZTEN UNTERSCHRIFT ROGER CASEMENTS VOR SEINER GEFANGENNAHME.

Rolf v. Hoerschelmann sc.

An insert from a German book that was used as evidence in a treason case against Sir Roger Casement, an Irish Republican sympathiser, caught attempting to smuggle German firearms into Ireland. His signature can clearly be seen on the document. The British government used a very loose interpretation of treason laws to convict and hang Casement on the 3rd of August 1916.

5th May, 1917

Die Karte, die wir hier wiedergeben, besitzt historischen Wert. Wir sehen auf ihr die letzte Unterschrift Roger Casements, bevor er an jenem Karfreitagmorgen, dem 21. April 1916, in McKenna's Fort (jetzt Casement's Fort genannt), bei Ardfert, an der Tralee-Bucht verhaftet wurde. Die Karte trägt das Datum vom 14. April, ist also genau eine Woche früher unterfertigt worden. Sie ist uns von dem Kommandanten des Schiffes, auf dem Casement die letzte tragische Heimfahrt unternahm, in liebenswürdigster Weise zur Verfügung gestellt worden. Casement hatte die Karte dem Kommandanten zur Erinnerung an die abenteuerliche Reise — die, wie er wohl wusste, auch seine letzte sein sollte — geschenkt.

Policewomen taking part in a restraining exercise in Brighton, Sussex. Women enrolled in the police force during the First World War to fill gaps in the ranks left by large numbers of policemen who enlisted in the British Armed Forces.
1918

This picture shows Kathleen Elsie Breaks who was found dead among sand dunes of the beach at Lytham St Annes, near Blackpool. Footprints, a revolver and blood stained gloves were found near the body. Her lover, Lieutenant Frederick Rothwell Holt, was convicted of her murder after the prosecution revealed he had persuaded her to make him the sole beneficiary of her considerable life insurance. Holt was hanged on the 13th of April 1920.

20th December, 1919

Police use a Ford Model T
car to regulate slow moving
traffic in the East End of
London.
12th October, 1920

Facing page: Remarkable scenes in Whitehall as the police
keep people from entering Downing Street on the day the
government declared a state of emergency because of a
miners' strike. The crowd's frustration led to a major riot in
which many people were injured.
18th October, 1920

Enoch Reid of Glasgow, seen posing for a photograph with his children, was charged with attempting to poison his wife.
20th December, 1920

Thomas Farrow (R) leaving
the Mansion House Police
Court after being charged
with conspiracy to defraud
the customers of Farrow's
Bank.

22nd December, 1920

Walter William Crotch
(second L) leaving the Guildhall
Police Court. Along with the
bank's owner, Thomas Farrow,
Crotch was sentenced to one
year of penal servitude for fraud
offences.
24th January, 1921

Reuben Bigland (second R) leaving Bow Street Magistrates'
Court after a libel case brought by his former associate
Horatio Bottomley. Bigland had printed a pamphlet in which he
described how Bottomley *"gulled poor subscribers to invest One
Pound Notes in his Great Victory War Bond Club"*. In a bizarre
twist, Rueben Bigland was acquitted and Bottomley was found
guilty of fraud and sentenced to seven years' imprisonment.
11th October, 1921

Ronald True, scion of a well-to-do family, murdered prostitute Olive Young. True had a history of mental health problems and was clearly unfit to stand trial, but was sentenced to the gallows. The Home Secretary Edward Shortt commuted the sentence to life in Broadmoor Prison for the Criminally Insane, provoking accusations that he was bowing to pressure from True's influential family. True died in Broadmoor in 1951.

1st May, 1922

Gerald Lee Bevan arriving at Waterloo Station accompanied by two detectives. Bevan, described in newspaper reports as a *"silver-tongued rogue and swindler"*, abused his position as the chairman of the City Equitable Fire Insurance Company to defraud tens of thousands of pounds. He was arrested in Vienna after fleeing Britain and eventually sentenced to seven years of penal servitude.

17th August, 1922

Frederick Bywaters arriving in court for his murder trial. Along with his lover Edith 'Edie' Thompson, he was convicted of stabbing to death her husband Percy Thompson who knew of their affair. On the 3rd of October 1922, Percy and Edie were returning from a concert in London, when Bywaters jumped out of a bush and killed Percy with a knife.

6th October, 1922

Frederick Bywaters (second L) in court during the Thompson-Bywaters case. Edith Thompson was also convicted of murder, despite the lack of evidence against her and the fact that over one million people signed a petition against her death sentence. They were both hanged on the 9th of January 1923. The famous executioner John Ellis committed suicide in 1932, after telling his friends that the gory hanging of Edith Thompson still haunted him.
6th December, 1922

Facing page: The crowd swarms onto the pitch before the first FA Cup Final to be played at Empire Stadium (later renamed Wembley Stadium). PC George Scorey and his grey horse Billy became famous for quelling the crowd. Bolton Wanderers beat West Ham United 2-0.

28th April, 1923

A crowd gathers outside Hailsham Police Court to catch a glimpse of Patrick Herbert Mahon who dismembered, and burned the severed head of, his mistress Emily Kaye at a bungalow near Eastbourne. He was sent to the gallows at Wandsworth Prison on the 2nd of September 1924.

7th May, 1924

Detective Sergeant Vanner and Detective Sergeant Sands
with 18 year old Arthur Henry Bishop, accused of murdering
Frank Edward Rix in Mayfair on the 7th of June 1925. Frank
Rix was a butler for Sir George Lloyd, a friend of Rudyard
Kipling. Bishop was hanged for the crime.
10th June, 1925

Oscar Slater (L) and the Reverend E P Philips (R) after Slater's
release from Barlinnie Gaol, Glasgow. Slater was convicted
in May 1909 of the murder of 82 year old Marion Gilchrist in
Glasgow, despite an excellent alibi. Supporters contacted
Sir Arthur Conan Doyle, the creator of the fictional detective
Sherlock Holmes, to ask for his assistance. Conan Doyle was
able to prove that Slater was innocent, but it took until 1927 for
him to be released.

27th May, 1927

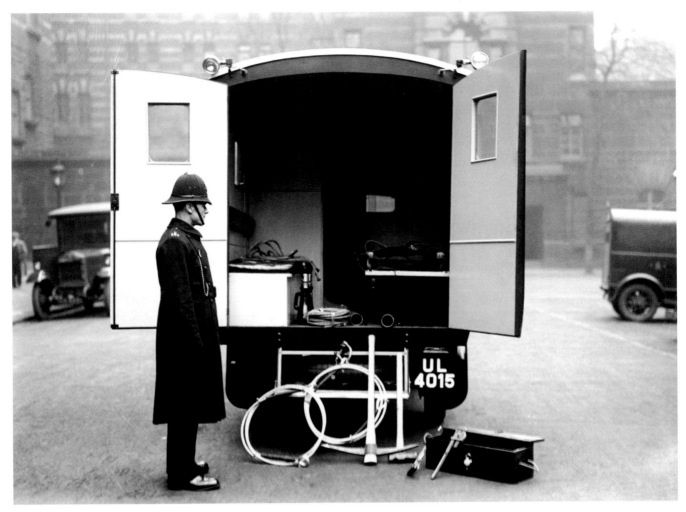

A police utility van.
27th March, 1929

Facing page: The new
police traffic control signs
on Brighton seafront.
5th August, 1928

A policeman directs traffic
with a new red safety light
attached to his belt.
29th November, 1929

Mr Justice Talbot, judge in the murder trial of Alfred Arthur Rouse in 1931. Rouse picked up a hitchhiker and burnt the car with the man inside. The case is unusual in legal history because Rouse was convicted of murdering a victim whose identity was never established. Rouse was hanged on the 10th of March 1931.

1930

Mounted policemen exit
Old Scotland Yard.
1st November, 1932

Facing page: A three-wheeled
BSA police car. Top speed
would have been around
50-60 mph.
1st March, 1932

Thames Police headquarters at Wapping. Launched in 1798, Thames Police was the first river-based division in the country.
7th September, 1934

Trainee policemen dash
to their cars at the Mobile
Police Training College at
Hendon, north London.
15th April, 1935

Skidding across a greased
track, a trainee policemen
practices at the Mobile
Police Training College at
Hendon, north London.
15th April, 1935

Trainee policeman receive instruction on safety using a model village at the Mobile Police Training College at Hendon, north London.

15th April, 1935

Police foil an assassination attempt by journalist Jerome
Bannigan (alias George Andrew McMahon) on King Edward
VIII. Confidential documents released in 2003 by the Public
Record Office detail how Bannigan had intended to shoot
himself in front of the King as he made his way back to
Buckingham Palace via Constitution Hill after reviewing the
Guards. Bannigan was sentenced to 12 months' hard labour.
16th July, 1936

A policeman charges into demonstrators with his truncheon during a march through London's East End by Sir Oswald Mosley's British Union of Fascists, known as the Blackshirts.
4th October, 1936

A mounted policeman falling with his horse during skirmishes
between the British Union of Fascists and anti-fascists,
many from the East End's predominantly Jewish and Irish
Catholic communities. Known as the Battle of Cable Street,
this disturbance was a major factor leading to the passage
of the Public Order Act 1936, that required police consent
for political marches and forbade the wearing of political
uniforms in public.
4th October, 1936

Sir Oswald Mosley, leader of the British Union of Fascists, addressing a meeting. Sir Oswald founded the 'Blackshirts' in 1932, but his wife, Lady Diana Mosley, was deemed more dangerous than her husband according to secret documents published in 2002 by the Public Record Office.

15th October, 1936

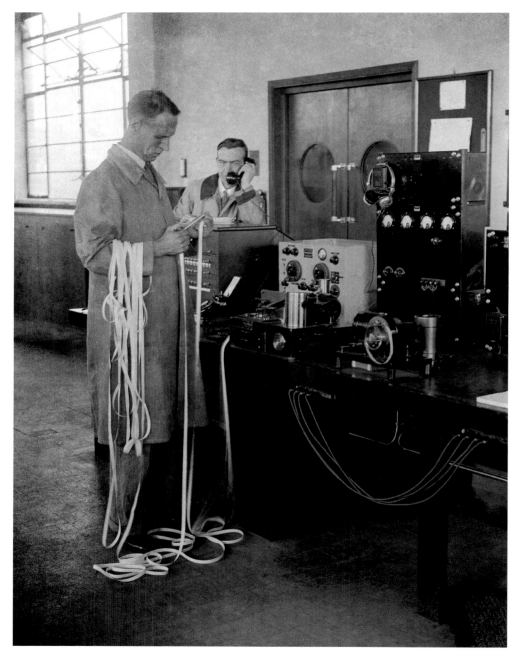

Facing page: Policemen with tin helmets and gas masks.
1939

The check-tape receiver of the West Wickham police radio transmitter.
23rd October, 1937

A police officer carefully scrutinising passes into the House of Commons during the first months of the Second World War.
13th December, 1939

PC Williams on duty
in London.
10th February, 1941

Crowds around Wandsworth Prison when William Joyce, known to radio listeners during the Second World War as 'Lord Haw-Haw', was executed for treason. Joyce was a Nazi propagandist who used to broadcast over the German radio network throughout the war.
3rd January, 1946

OFFENCES IN RELATION TO PRISONS

Military prisoners on the
roof of Aldershot detention
barracks while rioting about
overcrowding.
24th February, 1946

Neville George Clevely Heath (R) on his way to the West
London Police Court after being charged with the murder
of ex-WREN Doreen Marshall at Branksome Dean Chine,
Bournemouth. Heath had also sexually assaulted, murdered
and mutilated Margery Aimeé Brownell Gardner, a film extra,
on the 21st of June 1946. Prison doctors said that Heath was
a sadist, a sexual pervert and a psychopath. He was hanged
at Pentonville Prison on the 16th of October 1946.
29th July, 1946

A photograph showing a reconstruction of the house in Kensington to where John McMain Mudie was lured, tortured and killed. Thomas John Ley, who suspected Mudie of having an affair with his mistress Maggie Brooke, later disposed of the body in a Surrey chalk pit.
24th September, 1946

The back door to 5 Beaufort Gardens, Kensington, where John McMain Mudie was tortured and killed by Thomas John Ley and accomplice Lawrence John Smith in a case that became known as the Chalk Pit Murder. Lawrence was sentenced to life imprisonment and Ley, a former Australian government minister, was sent to Broadmoor Asylum for the Criminally Insane. He was said to be the richest person ever sent there.
24th September, 1946

Violet van der Elst, millionairess campaigner against capital punishment, at Pentonville Prison where she distributed leaflets against the execution of George Neville Clevely Heath who had brutally murdered two women. She died penniless after an unsuccessful political career in 1966, the year after capital punishment for murder was abolished.
16th October, 1946

Witness Mrs Brook (second L)
with her daughter after the trial
of the Chalk Pit Murder case.
24th March, 1947

Actress Eileen 'Gay' Gibson who was murdered on the high seas by deck steward James Camb. Eileen Gibson's body was pushed through a porthole of the liner *SS Durban* and never recovered.
25th October, 1947

Facing page: Policemen try to pick the winners during Derby Day at Epsom.
5th June, 1948

The mother of Eileen Gibson outside Winchester Assizes. James Camb was sentenced to life imprisonment for her murder. He was paroled in 1959, but while working as a head waiter in May 1967 he was convicted of sexually assaulting a 13 year old girl. He died in prison.
23rd March, 1947

The scene of the infamous 'Acid Bath Murders'. At a
ramshackle factory in Crawley, West Sussex, 39 year old
company director John George Haigh shot wealthy widow
Olive Durand-Deacon and disposed of her body in sulphuric
acid. While investigating the human sludge remains, three
gallstones and part of her dentures were found.
2nd March, 1949

John George Haigh at Horsham Courthouse, West Sussex, after being put on remand for the murder of Olivia Durand-Deacon. Police discovered she was the sixth victim in the so-called Acid Bath Murders.
11th March, 1949

John George Haigh, perpetrator of the Acid Bath Murders.
Dr Henry Yellowlees said during the trial that: *"the absolute
callous, cheerful, bland and almost friendly indifference of
the accused to the crimes which he freely admits having
committed is unique in my experience"*.
2nd April, 1949

Detective Sergeant Patrick Heslin (L) and Divisional
Detective Inspector Shelley Syms (second L) arriving at
Horsham Magistrates' Court to attend the trial of John
George Haig. He was hanged on the 10th of August 1949.
2nd April, 1949

Facing page: A policeman guiding children across a London road.
16th December, 1949

A crowd gathers outside the gates of Wandsworth Prison on the day John George Haigh was hanged for the Acid Bath Murders.
10th August, 1949

Shrouded in a raincoat, Thomas Philip George Stillwell, a
26 year old labourer of Offham, Sussex, before appearing at
Littlehampton Magistrates' Court charged with the murder of
Joan Mary Woodhouse, a 27 year old librarian from London.
31st August, 1950

Facing page: Metropolitan
police give 'safety first'
demonstrations to
schoolchildren.
19th September, 1950

Donald Maclean, a former British diplomat, was publicly exposed as a spy for the Russians in 1951. Maclean defected to Russia and lived there until he died in 1983.
1951

The Scottish Stone of Destiny (Stone of Scone), used for centuries in the coronation of Kings of Scotland, England and Britain, being removed from Arbroath Abbey, Forfarshire, by police. Three Scottish students stole the stone in protest from Westminster Abbey on Christmas morning 1950 and returned it to Scotland.

11th April, 1951

A policeman armed with a Sten gun covers the house in Chatham, Kent, where Alan Derek Poole was holed-up after fatally shooting a police officer. Poole, an army deserter, was killed by a police marksman during the siege.

6th June, 1951

The father of gunman Alan Derek Poole, shot dead by police, walks towards the man's weeping brother as his body is removed from the house in which he died.
6th June, 1951

Cambridge spy Guy Burgess, who fled to Russia with his friend and fellow spy Donald Maclean. For nearly five years their whereabouts was a mystery until they revealed themselves in Moscow in 1956.

8th June, 1951

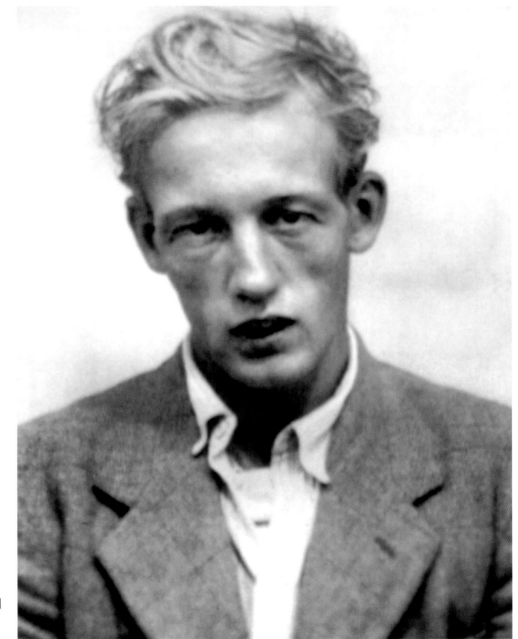

John Straffen, 21, who murdered five year old Linda Bowyer during an escape from Broadmoor, where he was serving a sentence passed the year before for the murders of Brenda Goddard, aged five, and Cicely Batstone, aged nine, in Bath. He was recaptured, tried and this time sentenced to death, but was reprieved.

30th April, 1952

Facing page: John Straffen, charged with murdering five year old Linda Bowyer. Straffen became Britain's longest serving prisoner, dying in jail on the 19th of November 2007.
2nd May, 1952

John Straffen leaving Winchester Crown Court after the first day's hearing. Straffen was sentenced to death by Mr Justice Cassells for killing three young girls. The then Home Secretary, Sir David Maxwell Fyfe, reduced the sentence to life imprisonment on the grounds that he was a 'feeble-minded person'.
21st July, 1952

A child's cycle and bundles of clothes used as evidence in the case against John Straffen.
21st July, 1952

Facing page: Murderer John Christie being led out of a prison van by police. In 1950, Timothy Evans was wrongfully hanged for the murder of his wife and baby. Three years later his neighbour John Christie, who had been a central prosecution witness at Evan's trial, confessed to killing eight female victims at 10 Rillington Place, Notting Hill, west London. The victims included Beryl Evans and her 14 month old baby. Christie, too, was hanged.
15th April, 1953

Murdered racing driver David
Blakely, who was killed by
his model girlfriend Ruth
Ellis. She became the last
woman to be hanged in
Britain.
19th April, 1955

Ruth Ellis, hanged at Holloway Prison on 13th July 1955 for gunning down her boyfriend David Blakely. Ellis's friend Jacqueline Dyer revealed during the trial that Blakely "*beat her unmercifully*".
28th April, 1955

A line of police keeps the crowd from approaching the gates of Holloway Prison in London as Ruth Ellis is executed for the murder of David Blakely. Solicitor Bernard de Maid told BBC Radio 4's *Today* programme that she should never have been put to death, because the killing was a true crime of passion.
13th July, 1955

Alone, the somewhat tragic figure of Violet Van Der Elst, an active campaigner against capital punishment, stands apart from police officers outside Holloway Prison in north London on the day Ruth Ellis was hanged. Ellis' death gave impetus to the anti-capital punishment lobby to continue to protest against executions.

13th July, 1955

Billy Hill, self-styled boss of the London underworld, attends court at the trial of Jack Comer, alias Jack Spot, charged with injuring Thomas Falco. Hill caused a sensation in the courtroom when he walked into the witness box and said: "*I am the boss of the Underworld*".
17th July, 1956

Officers from Lancashire
County Police using the
controversial new speed
radar gun.
25th July, 1957

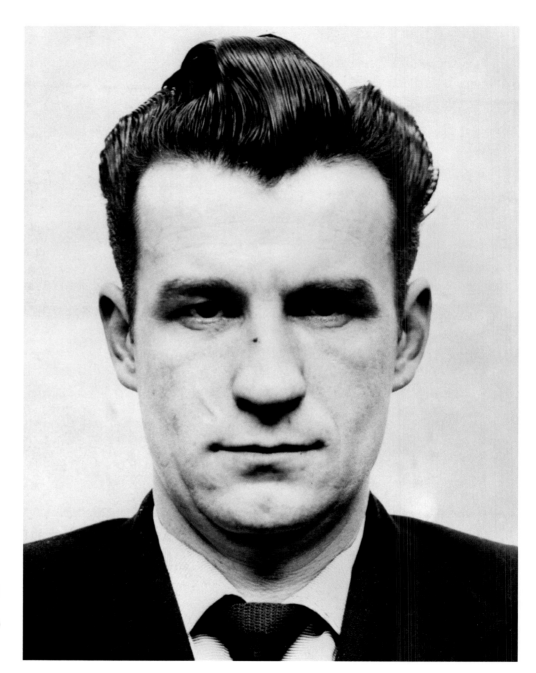

Lanarkshire woodworker Peter Thomas Anthony Manuel, 32, was sentenced to death for slaughtering seven people, including two 17 year old girls.
21st June, 1958

Underworld gangster Frank 'Mad Axeman' Mitchell, pictured in 1956, arriving at Wokingham Magistrates' Court where he was sentenced to life for robbery with violence. Mitchell fled HMP Dartmoor while on an outdoor working party, reputedly assisted by the Kray Twins. The notorious gangsters were also said to have been behind his murder several years later, but were acquitted. Mitchell's body was never found.
10th July, 1958

Police officers with dogs during renewed race rioting in London's Notting Hill. The events were sparked when white youths attacked Swedish woman Majbritt Morrison when they discovered she had a Jamaican husband.

1st September, 1958

Police walk along the edge of the pavement to ensure that the crowd keep moving at Notting Hill, London, where violence continues.
1st September, 1958

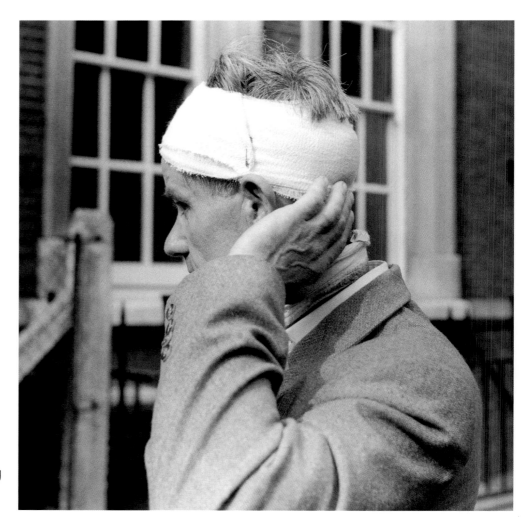

A man shows how he was injured during the riots in Notting Hill. Police arrested more than 140 people during two weeks of turmoil.
2nd September, 1958

A West Indian man and his white girlfriend walk through the streets of Notting Hill despite the threat from right-wing thugs following disturbances in the area.
2nd September, 1958

The Queen discusses some of the exhibits with Sir Anthony Blunt at the Courtauld Institute of Art in London. In 1979 Blunt, the Queen's Adviser on Art, was exposed as a Russian spy and part of the Cambridge Spy Ring.
19th February, 1959

Three female police officers
on lightweight motorcycles.
8th March, 1960

Facing page: Dr John Bodkin Adams leaving Hallam Street, London, after attending a public sitting of the General Medical Council Disciplinary Committee. Adams was convicted for fraud and suspected of being a serial killer. More than 160 of his patients, mostly in Eastbourne, East Sussex, died in suspicious circumstances over a ten-year period. Adams was tried and cleared of the murder of just one patient.
23rd November, 1960

Private Dennis Nilsen in 1961, serving as a cook in the British Army. Serial killer Nilsen was convicted in 1983 for six murders and two attempted murders. It is now known that he killed at least 15 men.
1961

The Morris Minor that
was used by James
Hanratty, who shot dead
Michael Gregsten and
raped his girlfriend Valerie
Storie on Deadman's Hill,
Bedfordshire.
23rd August, 1961

Men of the Royal Engineers use mine detectors in search of the weapon used by James Hanratty to shoot Michael Gregsten and Valerie Storie.

23rd August, 1961

Murderer James Hanratty, 25, with a raincoat over his head, seated between two police officers.
16th October, 1961

James Hanratty, who was hanged on the 4th of April, 1962 for killing Michael Gregsten and raping Valerie Storie.
1962

Justice Gorman, the judge at the trial of James Hanratty. Despite much evidence to the contrary, Hanratty was found guilty and executed. In 2001 his body was exhumed to extract DNA. It matched that found on the victims' possessions.

23rd January, 1962

Jack Spot (R) and Michael Goodman (L) as they leave London Airport for Dublin to shoot a film which has 'crime does not pay' as its theme. Jack 'Spot' Comer was a notorious Jewish gangster in London during the 1930s, 1940s and 1950s.

4th March, 1962

A study in expressions among more than 200 bystanders by the gates of Bedford Prison when James Hanratty was executed.
4th April, 1962

A London police van.
1st August, 1962

Ronnie Biggs, 35, jailed for 30 years for his part in the Great Train Robbery, was one of four prisoners that escaped from Wandsworth Prison. After serving 15 months of his sentence he fled to Rio de Janeiro where he lived until 2001. On his return to Britain Biggs was immediately imprisoned.
8th July, 1963

A photograph distributed to the press: (L–R) Bruce Richard Reynolds, Frances Reynolds, Barbara Maria Daly and John Thomas Daly, wanted in connection with the Great Train Robbery. Reynolds was the leader of the gang that made off with £2.6m.
1st August, 1963

Facing page: The coaches of the train involved in the Great Train Robbery. Most of the money stolen was never recovered.

10th August, 1963

A police car escorts the lorry and two Land Rovers, used to haul £2.6m of used bank notes stolen in the Great Train Robbery.

19th August, 1963

Facing page: A dramatic scene at the corner of Marchment Street and Coram Street, London, as Thomas French, 30, threatens to jump from a roof high above the streets of Bloomsbury, taking his infant son with him. The baby was taken from his arms by WPC Margaret Clelland and saved. Police restrained French after a fierce but short struggle.
3rd March, 1964

Brian Arthur Field and Leonard Dennis Field (no relation) arriving at court in Linslade, Buckinghamshire, after being charged with taking part in the £2.6m Great Train Robbery. Both were sentenced to 25 years in prison, later reduced to five years.
17th September, 1963

An assortment of modern
vehicles used by the
Metropolitan Police.
9th March, 1964

William Boal at Aylesbury, Buckinghamshire, accused of taking part in the Great Train Robbery. He was sentenced to 24 years in prison, later reduced to 14.
26th March, 1964

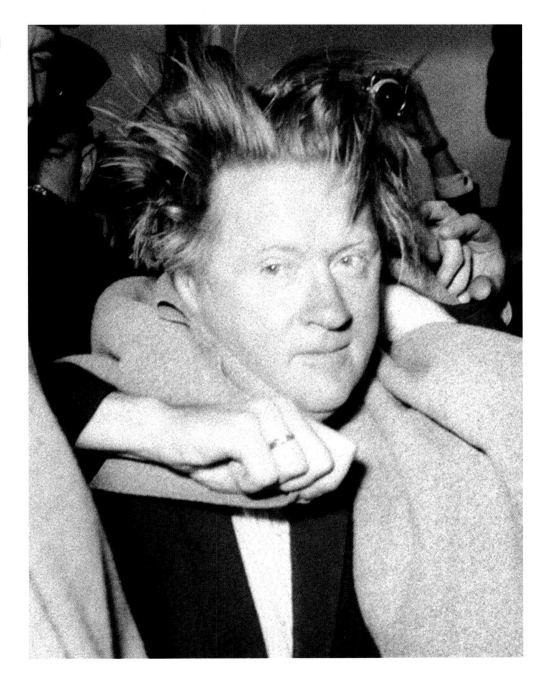

Charles Frederick Wilson, sentenced to 30 years for his part in the £2.6m Great Train Robbery, leaving Aylesbury court in Buckinghamshire. He escaped from Winson Green Prison in Birmingham on the 12th of August 1964 and went on the run for four years.

26th March, 1964

Clockwise from top left: Thomas William Wisbey, 33, a bookmaker, Douglas Gordon Goody, 34, a hairdresser, James Hussey, 30, painter and William Gered Boal, 50, an engineer who were part of the gang that carried out the Great Train Robbery.

26th March, 1964

Facing page: Safely
through the traffic outside
Buckingham Palace, mother
duck and her ducklings
march on, under police
escort, to St James' Park
and the peace of the lake.
4th May, 1964

Brighton police arresting
youths during fighting
between Mods and Rockers
on Brighton beach.
18th May, 1964

Police investigate a crime scene where the naked body of a woman was found strangled in Swyncombe, Brentford. The murderer was known to have killed six women in the Chiswick and Hammersmith areas of London. He was never caught, although a strong suspect in the case commited suicide just as the murders appeared to stop.
24th June, 1964

Interested onlookers watch from the promenade railings as police shepherd a large crowd of youths from the beach at Brighton on Bank Holiday Monday. Mass fights between Mods, Rockers and police erupted in seaside resorts throughout the summer of 1964, as intense rivalry between the motorcycling Rockers and the scooter-riding Mods led to violence.

June, 1964

Police mount a search of Saddleworth Moor in Yorkshire for the victims of Ian Brady and Myra Hindley. Five children, aged between 10 and 17 years, were raped and murdered by Brady, assisted by Hindley.
15th September, 1965

David Corbett holds a cheque for £500 given to him as a reward for finding the World Cup trophy. With him are his wife Jeanne and their dog Pickles, who found the world famous trophy in their garden. Pickles briefly became a national hero.
31st March, 1966

The three London police officers, (L–R) PC Geoffrey Fox, Temporary Detective Constable David Wombwell and Detective Sergeant Christopher Head, who were shot and killed in London by Harry Roberts, when they pulled his car over.

12th August, 1966

Police killer Harry Roberts who gunned down three unarmed officers in London. Roberts eluded a huge manhunt by hiding out for three months in Epping Forest. Roberts was sentenced to 30 years in prison.
18th August, 1966

Facing page: A police constable hands broken glass, collected from the terraces, to his sergeant after fighting broke out in the crowd during a game between West Ham United and Manchester United at Upton Park.
6th May, 1967

10 Rillington Place in London, scene of the John Christie murders in the early 1950s. Timothy Evans was wrongly convicted and hanged for two of these killings – the murder of his wife and child – which Christie later admitted. However, it wasn't until 1966 that the Brabin Report led to a posthumous partial pardon for the wrongly convicted Evans.
12th October, 1966

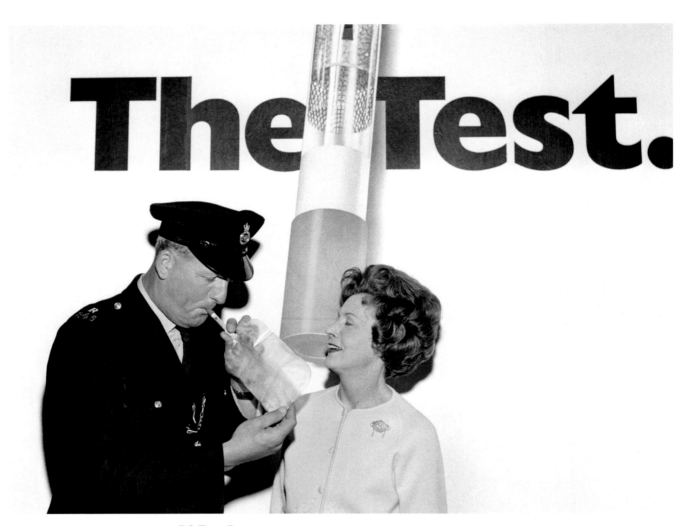

The Test.

PC Tony Burton
demonstrating the Alcotest
80 for the Transport
Secretary Barbara Castle,
as she launched a campaign
informing the public of the
new breathalyser law.
19th September, 1967

His face covered by a coat, Charles Wilson, handcuffed
to Detective Sergeant Ted Fuller (R) leaves an aircraft at
Heathrow Airport after returning from Canada where he was
in hiding after being convicted of taking part in the Great
Train Robbery.
28th January, 1968

Sislin Fay Allen, Britain's first
black policewoman.
15th February, 1968

Police officers move together in a tight line during a demonstration in Grosvenor Square, London, against the Vietnam War.
21st July, 1968

Facing page: Alert policemen take a peek over the hedge at two protestors in Grosvenor Square, home of the American Embassy, at a demonstration during a visit by United States President Richard Nixon.
24th February, 1969

Troops sprint from their barracks in Holywood, near Belfast, to board a truck to take up guard duty. Secret papers made public in 2000 revealed that the British government had no real intelligence about the IRA at the outbreak of 'The Troubles' in Northern Ireland.
22nd April, 1969

Facing page: A British Army soldier on lookout in the Falls Road area of Belfast.
15th August, 1969

Piara Singh Kenth, 30, from Kenya, the Metropolitan Police Force's new Sikh officer.
29th October, 1969

Two anti-apartheid
demonstrators who climbed
to the top of the goalposts
during the South African
Springboks rugby match at
Aberdeen.

2nd December, 1969

Police struggle with anti-apartheid protestors who had
invaded the pitch during the South African Springboks
rugby match against the North and Midlands Rugby team at
Linksfield Stadium, Aberdeen.
2nd December, 1969

Facing page: In front of a poster that reads "Britain Murdered Hanratty", anti-capital punishment campaigners John Lennon and Yoko Ono talk with Mr and Mrs James Hanratty, whose son James Hanratty was executed at Bedford Prison in 1962 after he was found guilty of the murder of Michael Gregsten and the rape and attempted murder of Gregsten's lover, Valerie Storey.

10th December, 1969

The Union of Santa Clauses, formed by American writer Ed Berman "*to protect the fantasies of children from exploitation*" and "*to get every Santa to refuse to work for a store which charges for its presents to the little ones*" called its first militant action outside Selfridges in London.

17th December, 1969

Timothy Franklin after his arrest for the murder of his girlfriend Tina Strauss. He killed her at their home in the village of North Otterington, Yorkshire, and buried her body in the garden. He was jailed for life.
8th March, 1971

A policeman grasps a young fan in a headlock after crowd trouble erupted before a match at Anfield between Liverpool and Manchester United.
20th August, 1971

A photograph showing the damage caused by an IRA bomb to the Post Office Tower in central London. Firemen can be seen clearing up debris on the 32nd floor, the sides of which are partially open to the elements.
31st October, 1971

Clearing up the debris that was hurled in all directions after a blast at the officers' mess of the 16th Parachute Brigade in Aldershot. Seven people were killed in the explosion. The IRA claimed it was in retaliation for the 'Bloody Sunday' shootings.

22nd February, 1972

Facing page: General Robert Ford, Britain's Commander of Land Forces in Northern Ireland, pictured in the Ainsworth Avenue area of Belfast, where he talked to Protestant UDA leaders during a confrontation between his troops and a crowd of UDA men. Ford was leading the forces at the time of the 'Bloody Sunday' massacre when British troops fired upon and killed 13 unarmed men on a civil rights march.
3rd July, 1972

Jethro Batt, who lost his hair while recovering from being poisoned by Graham Young. Young, who was fascinated by toxins from an early age, was convicted of murdering his stepmother in 1962. After a nine-year spell in Broadmoor he went on to kill two work colleagues. It is thought he poisoned more than 70 people.
20th June, 1972

Former architect John Poulson (foreground R) at Leeds Crown Court on corruption charges. Poulson used bribery and corrupt practices to ensure that his political contacts enabled him to receive lucrative contracts. The Conservative Home Secretary, Reginald Maudling, was forced to resign because he was closely implicated in the corruption trial. Poulson was sentenced to five years in prison (later increased to seven).

2nd October, 1973

Westminster Hall burns as emergency services tackle a blaze started when an incendiary device planted by the IRA exploded. Eleven people were injured.
17th June, 1974

A fan is escorted away by two police officers after fighting broke out between rival sets of supporters during a match between Cardiff City and Manchester United.
31st August, 1974

Four people were killed and more than 50 injured in a Provisional IRA bomb attack on the Horse and Groom in Guildford, a pub popular with army personnel. Gerry Conlon, Paul Hill, Patrick Armstrong and Carole Richardson were imprisoned for the attack, but their convictions were overturned 15 years later.

5th October, 1974

A woman comforts a bandaged casualty in an ambulance after two Birmingham pubs, The Tavern in the Town and the Mulberry Bush, were the target of IRA bomb attacks that killed a total of 21 people.

22nd November, 1974

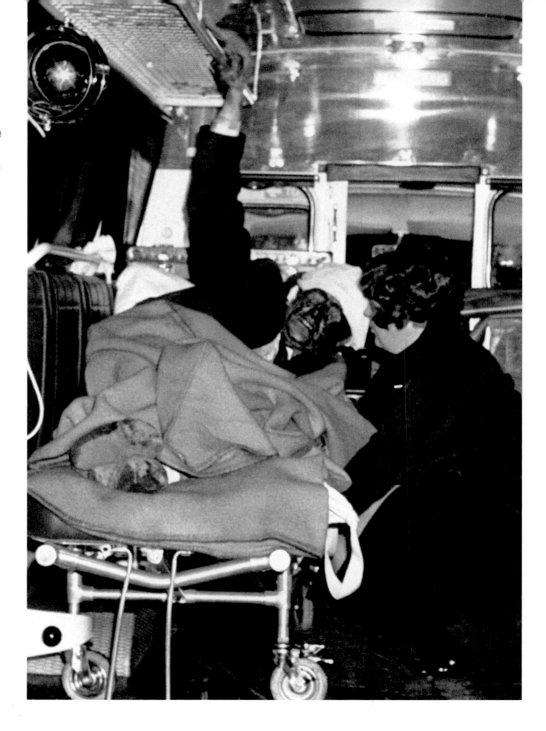

A portrait of 17 year old
Lesley Whittle, a missing
heiress, being posted at a
police station.
17th January, 1975

Police with tracker dogs
search waste ground
at Sedgley to look for
clues connected with the
kidnapping of Lesley Whittle.
14th February, 1975

Police raise a manhole cover at Bathpool Park, Kidsgrove, Staffordshire, where the body of Lesley Whittle, the missing heiress, was found. Donald Neilson, who had kidnapped and murdered the girl, was also found guilty of killing of three sub-postmasters in Post Office raids, and sentenced to life in prison.

9th March, 1975

A tent covers the manhole
where the body of Lesley
Whittle was found hanging
by a wire at the bottom of
a shaft.
11th March, 1975

The coffin of 17 year old Lesley Whittle, followed by mourners, led by Lesley's brother Ronald, makes its way through the snow-covered churchyard at the parish church of St Mary at Highley for her funeral.
14th March, 1975

This artist's impression of the serial killer Donald Neilson, also known as the 'Black Panther', was issued by police.

9th April, 1975

5' 7" 8' THIN BUILD . 36 38 YRS
WEARING FELT CAP. HAS DARK STAR
EYES. LONG NOSE. HIGH CHEEK B

Susan Maxwell-Scott leaving a public house in Westminster with her husband Ian. She was the last person to see Lord Lucan after the murder of his children's nanny in Belgravia. The official version states that he was intending to murder his wife but mistook her for the nanny, Sandra Rivett. Lord Lucan disappeared and was never found, being declared legally dead in 1999.

17th June, 1975

Police aim at a house in central London where the Balcombe Street gang, four highly trained IRA men, were holding a couple hostage. The dramatic siege saw policemen wielding guns on Britain's streets for the first time in such a public manner. The gang gave themselves up after a six-day stand-off when the SAS were called in.

8th December, 1975

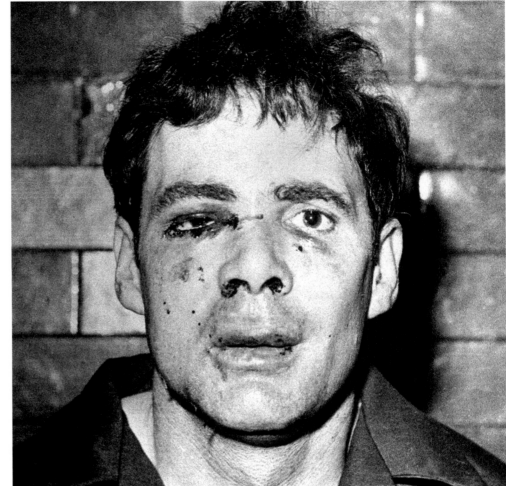

Donald Neilson, the serial killer, after his arrest in Rainworth, Nottinghamshire, where he received a severe beating from members of the public assisting in his arrest. He had kidnapped two police officers who stopped his car at gun point, but was eventually overpowered by the officers and members of the public.

12th December, 1975

Retired Commander Wallace
Harold Virgo, former head
of the Scotland Yard Murder
Squad, when he was one of
12 top Scotland Yard men
charged with conspiring to
corruptly receive monies and
other considerations from
pornographers.
1st March, 1976

Susan Mayor, of the costume department at Christie's, with Lord Lucan's coronet and robes which were auctioned to pay the missing peer's creditors.

23rd May, 1976

Weapons, equipment and clothing found by police in the possession of Donald Neilson. The collection includes two hoods with eyeholes, a sawn-off shotgun, a bandolier of cartridges and two knives.

1st June, 1976

A picture of murderer Donald Neilson during his National Service in the 1950s.
14th June, 1976

The complex drainage tunnels in Bathpool Park, Kidsgrove, where Lesley Whittle met her death at the hands of Donald Neilson, are sealed to guard against intruders.
1st July, 1976

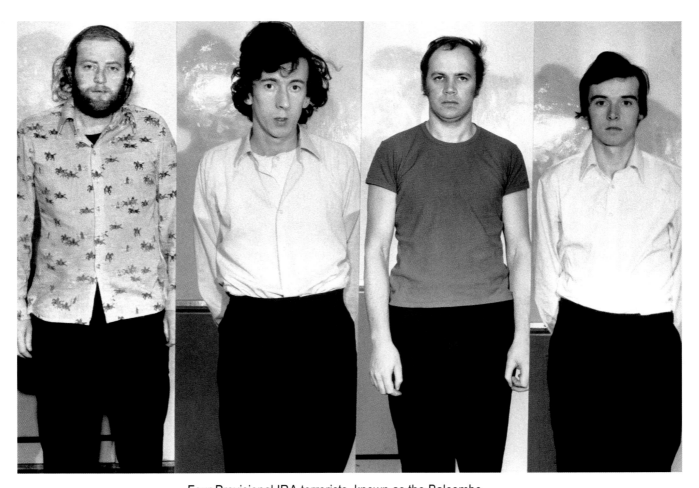

Four Provisional IRA terrorists, known as the Balcombe Street Gang, in a line up in London. (L–R) Hugh Doherty, Martin O'Connel, Edward Butler and Harry Duggan. Doherty received 11 life sentences, the rest received 12. They were released in 1999 as part of the Good Friday Agreement.
10th February, 1977

(L–R) Ex-Inspector Leslie Alton, Ex-Detective Constable Bernard Brown and Detective Sergeant David Hamer, three of the 'Porn Squad' who were accused at the Old Bailey of 27 counts of conspiracy and bribery.
2nd March, 1977

Facing page: A smoke bomb erupts around Union Jack carrying supporters of the National Front in north London as they clashed with anti-fascist campaigners.
23rd April, 1977

Peter Hain addressing fellow Anti-Nazi League supporters as they gathered at Seven Kings in London in preparation for a counter-canvass against the National Front electioneering campaign in Ilford. Peter Hain became Labour Member of Parliament for the Neath constituency in Wales.

25th February, 1978

Great Train Robber James
'Jimmy' White after his
release from prison.
25th April, 1978

Smoke drifting around a
gasholder during a fire,
started by an IRA incendiary
bomb, at the South-Eastern
Gas Board's Thames-Side
Works at Greenwich.
18th January, 1979

The mangled remains of the blue Vauxhall car on the underground car park ramp at the House of Commons after being ripped apart by a bomb blast which killed Airey Neave MP, 63 year old Conservative spokesman on Northern Ireland. Both the Provisional IRA and the Irish National Liberation Army (INLA) claimed responsibility for the attack.

30th March, 1979

The Great Train Robbers (L–R) Buster Edwards, Tommy Wiseby, Jim White, Bruce Reynolds, Roger Cordrey, Charles Wilson and Jim Hussey, reunite for the launch of the book *The Great Train Robbers – Their Story* that recalls the events surrounding the £2.6m heist that took place in 1963.
16th July, 1979

Prince Charles reads the lesson during the funeral service of Lord Mountbatten in Westminster Abbey. Lord Mountbatten was assassinated by the Provisional IRA, who planted a bomb in his boat at Mullaghmore, County Sligo in Ireland.
5th September, 1979

Facing page: Youths during riots in Bristol's St Paul's district in which at least 19 policemen were injured. Shops were looted, buildings and cars were set on fire during the disturbances. The violence erupted after a police drugs raid on the Black and White cafe.
2nd April, 1980

A wrecked shop in Ashley Road, Bristol, one of the targets during the rioting in Bristol's St Paul's district by young people from the deprived area.
3rd April, 1980

Members of the British Movement hold up a White Power
banner and give Nazi salutes, during a march from Hyde
Park, London, to Paddington Recreation Ground. The British
Movement was a splinter group of the National Front.
23rd November, 1980

Police investigate the scene
of a killing in Leeds that was
suspected of being the work
of the Yorkshire Ripper.
28th November, 1980

Serial killer Peter Sutcliffe, also known as the Yorkshire Ripper, with his wife Sonia. Sutcliffe was convicted for killing 13 women after a six-year search and sent to jail for life.

1st December, 1980

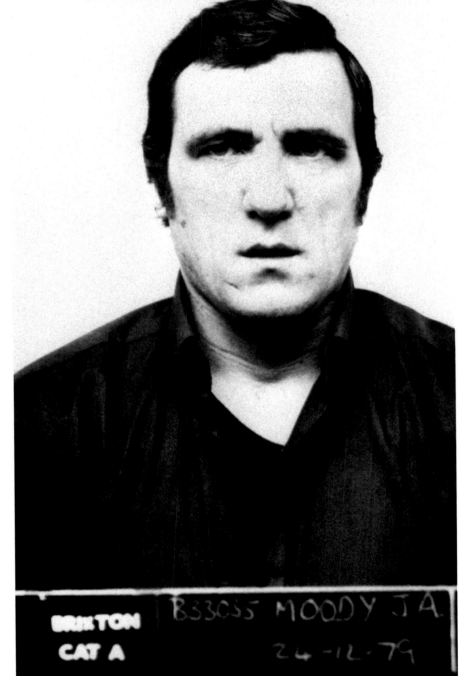

James Alfred Moody was one of the most feared hit men in London and Northern Ireland. He was due to appear in the Old Bailey after being arrested for armed robbery, but escaped from HM Prison Brixton along with Gerard Tuite, who had persuaded him to become an assassin for the Provisional IRA. In 1993 he was shot dead by an unknown gunman.
16th December, 1980

A police van on fire during riots in the deprived area of
Brixton, south London. Trouble started when police helped a
black youth who had been stabbed: rumours rapidly spread
that the youth died from police brutality.
11th April, 1981

A police officer, blood streaming from a head wound, being helped away by colleagues in Brixton during renewed fighting with youths. The area's residents were angered by a new operation to crack down on crime by employing stop and search tactics.

11th April, 1981

Facing page: An injured policeman in Brixton during the violence that engulfed the area for several nights.
11th April, 1981

A black youth confronts a senior police officer during the disturbances in Brixton, south London.
11th April, 1981

A police officer steers a toddler to safety in Brixton during riots.
11th April, 1981

Bradford lorry driver Peter
Sutcliffe, under cover of a
blanket, after being charged
with the murder of 13 women
and the attempted murder
of seven others. He was
convicted and sentenced to
life in prison.
22nd May, 1981

The aftermath of a night of violent rioting in the Toxteth district of Liverpool. The disturbances were sparked after the perceived heavy-handed arrest of Leroy Alphonse Cooper: long standing tensions between the police and youths boiled over into violence.

5th July, 1981

A column of police advance behind riot shields during serious fighting in Liverpool. One person died and more than 1,000 police officers were claimed to have been injured during nine days of violence. The police were accused of heavy-handedness and planting drugs during stop and search sweeps.

5th July, 1981

Teenagers survey the devastation following a second night of violent rioting in the Toxteth district of Liverpool. More than 500 buildings were destroyed during the mayhem.
6th July, 1981

Facing page: A moment of calm during the Toxteth riots. The Merseyside police had a poor reputation within the black community at the time.
7th July, 1981

Armed with riot shields, police huddle together for protection as violence again flared in Brixton. Between 200 and 400 youths were on the rampage. Rioters smashed shop windows in the Brixton Road and began looting.
10th July, 1981

Facing page: A police car blazes in Brixton.
10th July, 1981

The scene outside the Liverpool home of David Moore before his funeral. Disabled David, aged 23, was hit by a police Land Rover which was chasing rioters across waste ground in the Toxteth area of Liverpool.
10th August, 1981

Police and firemen at the still-smouldering bandstand in
Regents Park, London, following the IRA bomb blast that
killed six people and left many others seriously injured during
a performance by the Royal Green Jackets Band.
20th July, 1982

Gangster Ronnie Kray (second R) arrives under heavy guard at Chingford Old Church for the funeral of his mother, Violet Kray. Ronnie was brought from Broadmoor and twin Reggie from Parkhurst Prison, Isle of Wight, where they served life sentences for murder.
11th August, 1982

The Droppin' Well pub in Londonderry, Northern Ireland, after an Irish National Liberation Army bomb killed 11 soldiers and six civilians.
7th December, 1982

Police investigating human remains found in a drain at the house of Dennis Nilsen in Muswell Hill, London, after he suddenly admitted to killing 15 young men between 1978 and 1983.
10th February, 1983

Police dig in the back garden of a house at Melrose Avenue, Willesden, London. Dennis Nilsen is thought to have strangled his first victim at a flat there in 1976. Nilsen burned several of his victims on bonfires in the garden.

13th February, 1983

37 year old Dennis Andrew
Nilsen (R), handcuffed to
a police officer, arrives at
Highgate Magistrates' Court
for killing Stephen Sinclair
on the 26th of January 1983.
Sinclair was dismembered
after falling into a heroin and
alcohol induced stupor. It
was Nilsen's 15th murder.
24th March, 1983

The scene outside the Brinks Mat security warehouse on the Heathrow Industrial Trading Estate, where armed raiders got away with £26m in pure gold bullion. Staff inside were handcuffed and petrol was poured over them.
26th November, 1983

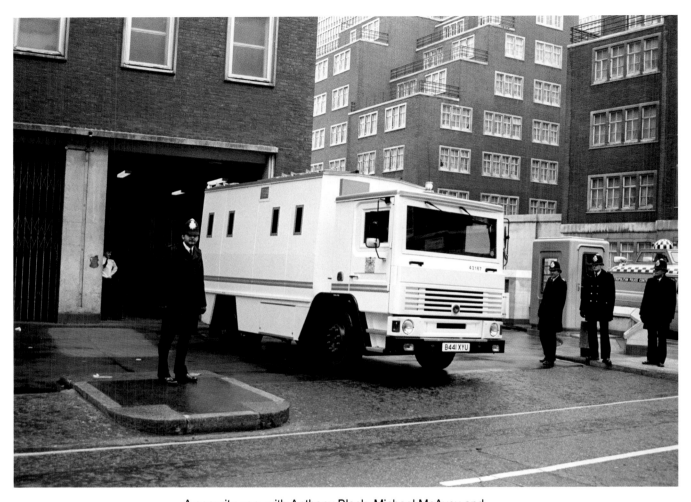

A security van, with Anthony Black, Michael McAvoy and Brian Robinson, leaves the Old Bailey during the trial of the men accused of the £26m gold bullion robbery at the Brinks Mat warehouse. Robinson and McAvoy were sentenced to 25 years in prison, Black to six years and served three.
28th November, 1983

Commander Frank Cater (L), Detective Superintendent Mervyn Atkinson (second L) and Deputy Assistant Commander David Powis (R) display two types of boxes in which £26m of gold bullion was wrapped, a bag used to hood a security guard and a photograph of the types of vans believed to have been used in the Brinks Mat robbery. It has been suggested that anyone wearing gold jewellery bought in the UK after 1983 is probably wearing Brinks Mat gold.

29th November, 1983

Facing page: A Provisional IRA bomb ripped through the Grand Hotel in Brighton during the Conservative Party conference in 1984. The blast killed five people and injured 34 more, including government minister Norman Tebbit. Prime Minister Margaret Thatcher was unscathed.

12th October, 1984

Robert Maxwell, Chairman of the Mirror Group Newspapers, in his office. The media mogul defrauded millions of pensioners who invested in his pension fund. He died while under investigation for fraud, on the 5th of November 1991, after falling overboard from his luxury yacht. The official verdict was accidental drowning, though some people have suggested that he may have committed suicide, and others that he was murdered.

1st August, 1984

GRAND

Scene at the Grand Hotel, Brighton, after a bomb explosion during the Conservative Party conference. Convicted bomber Patrick Magee served 14 years in prison before being released under the Good Friday Agreement in 1999.

12th October, 1984

Firemen working in the Grand Hotel where victims of the Provisional IRA bomb were found among the debris of the collapsed floors. The IRA released a statement saying: "*Mrs Thatcher will now realise that Britain cannot occupy our country and torture our prisoners and shoot our people in their own streets and get away with it*".

12th October, 1984

An IRA bomb attack in Dulwich, south London, where Lieutenant General Sir Stuart Pringle, Commandant-General of the Royal Marines, was critically injured in a blast as he drove his car away from his home.
13th February, 1985

Pitched battles between police and fans at Luton Town's Kenilworth Road ground after Luton beat Millwall 1-0 in the sixth round of the FA Cup.
14th March, 1985

Facing page: An investigation into a fire that gutted Lozells Road Post Office in the Handsworth area of Birmingham after fighting between police and some of the area's residents. It began when a man was arrested near the Acapulco Café and a raid was carried out on the Villa Cross pub.
10th September, 1985

The remains of a burnt-out car and litter lie strewn across the pavement in the Handsworth area of Birmingham. Two people were killed, two left unaccounted for and 35 injured over three nights of rioting.
10th September, 1985

Daylight reveals the full extent of the devastation in the
Handsworth area of Birmingham as two policemen survey
fire-gutted buildings following the violence.
10th September, 1985

A building consumed by fire on the corner of Gresham Road in Brixton, south London, after more upheaval. A shooting incident involving the police was blamed for the renewal of violence.

28th September, 1985

Facing page: Truncheons at the ready, police officers tackle unruly fans of Glasgow Rangers at White Hart Lane ground, London, where Tottenham Hotspur met Rangers in a testimonial football match for Paul Miller.
2nd August, 1986

Police in riot gear during the Broadwater Farm riot in Tottenham, north London. Winston Silcott was convicted of the murder of PC Keith Blakelock, who died during the clashes, but the decision was overturned in 1987 on appeal because of 'unsafe' police evidence.
6th October, 1985

Jeweller John Palmer at his home in Battlefields, Lanadown near Bath with his wife Marnia. The Terry's All Gold Easter egg was presented to them by the press. Palmer was acquitted at the Old Bailey on charges of handling gold stolen in the Brinks Mat £26m bullion robbery. None of the gold was ever recovered.

2nd April, 1987

Jeffrey Archer and his wife Mary leaving the rear entrance of the High Court, in London, after winning record damages of £500,000 in a libel action against *The Star* newspaper which alleged that he had slept with a prostitute. On the 19th of July 2001, Archer was found guilty of perjury and perverting the course of justice at the 1987 trial. He was sentenced to four years' imprisonment.

24th July, 1987

A police marksman espies a spent cartridge on the road in Hungerford after Michael Ryan went on the rampage with semi-automatic rifles and a handgun. He shot and killed 16 people including his mother.

19th August, 1987

Police marksmen in blue berets
and protective clothing leave a
van in Hungerford.
19th August, 1987

The burnt out shell of
Dorothy Ryan's house,
where Michael Ryan
murdered his 60 year old
mother. He randomly killed
another 15 people before
turning the gun on himself.
20th August, 1987

Margery Jackson receives treatment from ward sister Omy Ternowa in Barbury Ward at Princess Margaret Hospital, Swindon, after being wounded by Michael Ryan.
20th August, 1987

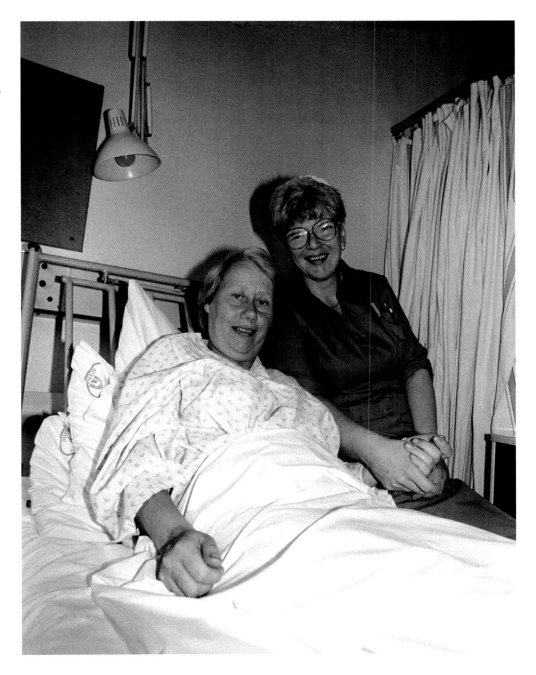

Distraught relatives leave the parish church of St Lawrence in Hungerford after an emotional Holy Communion service following the massacre of 16 townspeople by crazed gunman Michael Ryan. The event led to the introduction of the Firearms (Amendment) Act 1988, banning ownership of semi-automatic rifles and restricting the use of shotguns.
23rd August, 1987

Chief Inspector Laurie (L) and PC Colin Lilley (R) hold the weapons used by Hungerford killer Michael Ryan. Included in the stash were an Italian semi-automatic 9mm Beretta pistol, 30 calibre M1 semi-automatic carbine and a Chinese-made 'Type 56' copy of a semi-automatic Kalashnikov rifle. All were legally obtained and licensed to Ryan.

24th September, 1987

Mourners panic at Milltown Cemetery, Belfast, after a gun and bomb attack by Michael Stone which left three people dead and four seriously injured during the funerals of three IRA members shot dead in Gibraltar. Sources said that leading loyalist Michael Stone entered the building, shouting: "*No surrender*".
16th March, 1988

Rival fans fight at Wembley where England beat Scotland 1-0 in a Rous Cup match.
21st May, 1988

The wrecked nose section of Pan-Am Boeing 747 lies in a
Scottish field at Lockerbie, after the plane, which had been
flying from Frankfurt to New York, was blown apart by a
terrorist bomb killing all 259 passengers and 11 people on
the ground.
22nd December, 1988

Police officers investigating the wreckage of Pan-Am Flight 103. Former Libyan intelligence officer Abdelbaset Ali Mohmed Al Megrahi was found guilty of carrying out mass murder at a specially convened Scottish court in the Netherlands.

22nd December, 1988

Police officers among debris
left in the Scottish town of
Lockerbie after a Pan-Am
jumbo jet exploded mid-air
and crashed in flames onto
the market town.
23rd December, 1988

A cap and bugle at the scene of an IRA bomb blast at the Royal Marines School of Music at the Walmer Barracks, Deal, Kent. Eleven people were killed when the reception centre was torn apart.

22nd September, 1989

A protester is led away
by police officers during
the poll tax riots around
Trafalgar Square, London.
The disturbances are widely
considered to be the catalyst
that led to the downfall of
Prime Minister Margaret
Thatcher eight months later.
31st March, 1990

Masked prisoners at Strangeways Prison in Manchester hang a 'No Dead' message from a burnt out window. During 25 days of violence, one prisoner was killed, 147 prison officers and 47 prisoners injured.

2nd April, 1990

Anxious moments on the roof of Strangeways Prison,
Manchester, as a hostage with his hands tied is displayed
by hooded prisoners, with a noose hanging behind him.
Prisoners were demonstrating against overcrowded
conditions in the Victorian penal institution.
3rd April, 1990

Defiant prisoners raise clenched fists and wave on the rooftop of Strangeways Prison. The violence sparked disturbances in other prisons across Britain. The Woolf Report, following a public inquiry, said that conditions had become intolerable and that the prison system should undergo major reform.

4th April, 1990

A white van burns outside the Banqueting House in Whitehall after an attempted mortar bomb attack on Downing Street. One bomb exploded in the back yard of the Prime Minister's residence while John Major chaired a war cabinet.

7th February, 1991

Former nurse Beverley Allitt is driven away from Grantham Magistrates' Court after her trial for killing four children and attempting to murder nine others on the children's ward of Grantham and Kesteven Hospital. Known as 'the Angel of Death', Allitt, 31, received 13 life sentences.

28th November, 1991

St Mary's Axe in London
in the aftermath of an IRA
bomb blast.
11th April, 1992

The crater left by an IRA
bomb blast in St Mary's Axe
in the City of London.
14th April, 1992

Police divers search Queens Mere pond on Wimbledon Common in their hunt for the weapon used in the murder of young mother Rachel Nickell. She was raped and stabbed 49 times in front of her two year old son. Colin Stagg was arrested and charged, but finally acquitted. The case was reopened in 2006 when Robert Napper, remanded in Broadmoor for the murder of Samantha Bisset and her four year old daughter, admitted the attack.

20th July, 1992

Colin Stagg after he was charged with indecent exposure on Wimbledon common.
21st September, 1992

Facing page: Deserted streets filled with wreckage surround the Hong Kong and Shanghai Bank in Bishopsgate, London, after an IRA bomb attack. One person was killed and more than 40 injured.
24th April, 1993

A huge crater is left in the road at Bishopsgate in the City of London following an explosion. The bomb, made using a ton of fertiliser, was hidden in a tipper truck.
24th April, 1993

Kidnap victim Stephanie Slater arrives at Nottingham Crown Court to give evidence against her kidnapper, Michael Sams. Sams was convicted and later also found guilty of the murder of Julie Dart.
17th June, 1993

Michael Sams' home in Sutton-on-Trent. Sams was found guilty of kidnapping and raping Stephanie Slater and of the murder of Julie Dart.
8th July, 1993

Police officer DC Wayne holds a nailed board and knife used by Michael Sams to threaten abducted estate agent Stephanie Slater. Sams kept her captive in a makeshift coffin for eight days before releasing her for ransom money. Sams was also convicted of the murder of 18 year old Julie Dart.

8th July, 1993

Police sift through soil as they continue to find bodies buried in the garden of Fred West's former home in Gloucester. West was charged with the murders of 10 women.
27th April, 1994

Fred West leaving
Gloucester Magistrates'
Court. Along with his wife
Rosemary, he tortured,
raped and murdered at least
12 young women, mostly at
their home in Gloucester.
West hanged himself on
the 1st of January 1995 at
Winston Green Prison in
Birmingham.
28th July, 1994

Charlie Kray, the elder brother of London's Kray twins, at Maidstone Prison after visiting Reggie following the death of Ronnie, aged 61. Charlie Kray died aged 73 while serving a 12 year jail sentence for masterminding a £39m cocaine deal. Reggie was released from prison in 2000 on compassionate grounds, to die at home from cancer.
18th March, 1995

Doreen and Neville Lawrence outside Belmarsh Magistrates'
Court, south London, for the first day of the family's private
prosecution accusing four men of killing of their son Stephen.
Stephen Lawrence, 18, was stabbed to death at a bus stop in
Eltham, east London on the 22nd April 1993. The Lawrences
exposed the Metropolitan Police's shortcomings in their son's
investigation and they continue to speak on racial inequality
in Britain.

23rd August, 1995

Rosemary West after she had been imprisoned for life on ten counts of murder with Fred West, including that of her daughter Heather, 16, stepdaughter Charmaine, 8, and lodger Shirley Ann Robinson.

22nd November, 1995

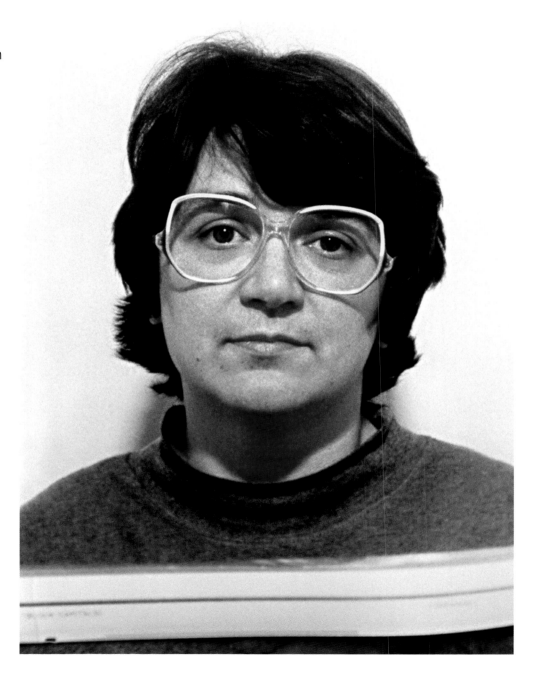

Police in riot gear watch a burning car during riots in Brixton, south London. Triggered by the death of 26 year old Wayne Douglas in police custody, tension erupted with participants destroying property and vehicles.
14th December, 1995

Convicted child-killer Robert Black who kidnapped, raped and murdered three girls during the 1980s. He is also suspected of involvement in a number of unsolved child murders throughout Europe, dating back to the 1970s.
2nd January, 1996

The sons of the late media tycoon Robert Maxwell, Kevin (third R) and Ian (second R), arrive at Chichester Rents Court charged with conspiracy to defraud pensioners. The case was brought against the two men when Robert Maxwell's business collapsed and it emerged that £400m was missing from pension funds. The brothers were later cleared of any criminal wrongdoing. Robert Maxwell died after falling from his yacht in 1991.

8th January, 1996

Philip Lawrence's family walk behind his coffin at Ealing Abbey in London. The headmaster was stabbed to death at his school gates as he tried to stop a gang fight involving one of his pupils. Lawrence was posthumously awarded the Queen's Gallantry medal in 1997.

16th February, 1996

Sixteen red roses stand
close to the gates of
Dunblane Primary School,
representing the young
children who were shot
dead by gunman Thomas
Hamilton.
14th March, 1996

A policeman stands watch over the school gymnasium where 16 children and their teacher were killed by crazed gunman Thomas Hamilton in Dunblane, Scotland.
14th March, 1996

The scene where 21 year old Stephen Cameron was stabbed to death in front of his fiancée on an M25 slip road. Kenneth Noye, out of 'road rage', stabbed Cameron with a knife he kept in the car. Twenty-two people witnessed the attack and Noye was jailed for life.

19th May, 1996

Police officers search a cornfield near the spot where Lin
Russell and her daughters Josephine and Megan were
brutally attacked while walking home from their school in an
idyllic area of Kent. Megan and her mother were both killed.
12th July, 1996

Fred and Rose West's former house at 25 Cromwell Street,
Gloucester is demolished. Known as the 'House of Horrors',
the community decided to demolish the site and replace
it with a green walkway in an attempt to move on from its
grisly past. The Wests murdered at least 12 young women,
including their daughter Heather who they buried underneath
the front porch.

11th October, 1996

An eerily quaint photograph
of serial killers Fred and
Rosemary West.
19th April, 1997

Michael Hickey outside the Royal Courts of Justice in
London at the start of an appeal against the sentences of
the 'Bridgewater Four'. Jim Robinson, Michael Hickey and
Vincent Hickey were convicted of the 1979 murder
of newsboy Carl Bridgewater. All were eventually acquitted
after the Court of Appeal judged the trail to be unfair.
21st April, 1997

Facing page: Loyalist paramilitary prisoner Michael Stone
stands inside the high security Maze Prison in Northern
Ireland. He was jailed for a series of murders, including an
attack on mourners attending the Milltown Cemetery funeral
for the three IRA terrorists shot dead by the SAS in Gibraltar
in March 1988.
8th January, 1998

Maria Dingwall Bentley, niece of the teenager Derek Bentley who was hanged in 1953, outside the High Court. The Lord Chief Justice, Lord Bingham, Lord Justice Kennedy and Justice Collins, quashed the murder conviction following a three-day hearing. Derek Bentley, who at the time was 19 but had a mental age of 11, was convicted in 1952 of murdering a policeman during an attempted burglary. His 16 year old accomplice fired the gun.

20th July, 1998

A prisoner walks down a corridor watched by an officer at
Feltham Young Offenders Institution in London. In a report
by the Chief Inspector of Prisons, Feltham was said to be an
affront to civilisation, guilty of institutionalised neglect, with
youngsters spending up to 22 hours a day in filthy, cold cells
with nothing to do.
25th March, 1999

A *Weston & Somerset Mercury* billboard, the paper where BBC presenter Jill Dando started her journalistic career, displays news of her death. Jill Dando was shot dead outside her home in Gowan Avenue, Fulham, London.
26th April, 1999

The Fulham home of TV presenter Jill Dando who was shot dead on her doorstep. Initially Barry George, a man suffering from mental disorders, was convicted of her murder. The verdict was eventually overturned on appeal and in 2008 George was acquitted of the murder. To date, no one has been brought to justice for the killing.

26th April, 1999

Make: SF FIREARMS
Model: MAC 10
Type: sub machine gun
Calibre: 9 millimetre PARABELLUM

Make: GLOCK
Model: 21
Type: self loading pistol
Calibre: .45 AUTO

Make: IMI
Model: DESERT EAGLE
Type: self loading pistol
Calibre: .357 MAGNUM

Make: CHINESE
Model: TYPE 54 – 1
Type: self loading pistol
Calibre: 7.62 millimetre TOKAREV
also found in reactivated form in 9 millimetre
PARABELLUM calibre.

Make: ENGLISH
Type: sawn off shotgun
12 bore

Make: WALTHER
Model: PPK / S
Type: self loading pistol
Calibre: 9 millimetre SHORT

Make: ITALIAN
Model: DERRINGER
Type: double – barrelled pistol
Calibre: .22 RIMFIRE
converted from a blank firing gun

Make: SMITH & WESSON
Model: 30 –1
Type: revolver
Calibre: .32 S & W

Make: MAB
Model: D
Type: self loading pistol
Calibre: .32 AUTO

Make: BROWNING
Model: HIGH POWER
Type: self loading pistol
Calibre: 9 millimetre PARABELLUM

An impressive haul of guns, on display at New Scotland Yard, commonly carried by gang members. This cache includes a MAC-10 that is capable of firing 10 rounds per second. Also exhibited are sawn-off shotguns and pistols, more common weapons.
20th October, 1999

LIVE AND LET LIVE

The Oldham riots in Greater Manchester. Hundreds of rioters armed with bricks and petrol bombs fought with police. The Asian neighbourhood of Glodwick saw the worst of the violence with cars torched and windows smashed.
27th May, 2001

Dame Janet Smith starts proceedings for the Shipman Inquiry held at Manchester Town Hall. Family GP Harold Shipman was found guilty of murdering 15 of his patients and thought to be responsible for the deaths of 618 more, making him one of the world's most prolific serial killers. Shipman administered lethal doses of diamorphine to his elderly patients, and in one instance forged a will, in an attempt to inherit £386,000.

20th June, 2001

Facing page: Smoke billows from a burning barricade on Abbey Street in Bradford as the Asian community and police clash after a day of violence in the city. The violence escalated in the Mannigham area of the city, where police were pelted with bricks, bottles and petrol bombs.

7th July, 2001

Police swoop on The Flower of Kent pub in Lewisham during 'Operation Vezere', an attempt to combat gun use. The week-long operation resulted in 50 arrests connected to drug dealing and organised crime within the area.
22nd October, 2004

Facing page: Police cordon the scene where wealthy city banker John Monckton and his wife were stabbed. Two men forced their way into the couple's Chelsea home in a violent attempted robbery. Mr Monckton died of knife injuries. The couple's nine year old daughter was upstairs when the attack took place and made the 999 call.
30th November, 2004

A woman leaves Edgware Road tube station with a protective burn mask after the July 2005 London suicide bombings. The city suffered four explosions at Russell Square, Aldgate and Edgware Road tube stations and on a bus in Tavistock Square. Fifty-two people were killed and 700 were injured.

7th July, 2005

A wounded survivor of
the Edgware Road tube
station explosion walks
away stunned.
7th July, 2005

Commuters surge towards Liverpool Street Station as it re-opens after a terrorist attack. The explosions shook Londoners' sense of safety as crowded public transport was targeted.
7th July, 2005

Police stand guard over a cordon in Beeston, near Leeds, after officers raided five residential premises in West Yorkshire in connection with the London bombings.
12th July, 2005

Facing page: Thousands of people gather at Trafalgar Square for a vigil to remember the victims of the London terror attacks.
14th July, 2005

Having first been winched out of the tunnel at Edgware Road station, the mangled carriage where seven people died from one of four terrorist bombs is transferred to a lorry, later to undergo forensic investigation.
19th July, 2005

A Queen's Park Rangers youth team member who played with Kiyan Prince, pays tribute to the slain 15 year old. A gifted young athlete, Kiyan was fatally stabbed as he tried to break up a fight outside his school in Edgware, north London.
19th May, 2006

Facing page: Forensics officers search outside a house in Trimley St Martin, Suffolk, following the arrest of Steve Wright. Wright was found guilty of murdering five women in Ipswich. The women had worked as prostitutes and were aged between 19 and 29.
19th December, 2006

The jury in the Steve Wright trial visit Hintlesham Fisheries where the body of 25 year old Gemma Adams was found. Over a ten day period, Wright systematically strangled five women and dumped them naked in countryside.
21st January, 2008

A West Yorkshire Police search team break ice on a lake close to the Dewsbury home of nine year old Shannon Matthews. After a 24 day disappearance, it was discovered that Shannon's mother and boyfriend had drugged and hidden the girl in a deceitful plot to make money.
20th February, 2008

Searching close to the home
of Shannon Matthews,
Dewsbury Police comb
the area. Shannon's
disappearance cost the
county £3.2m in police costs.
21st February, 2008

Residents of Dewsbury
fear the worst for Shannon
Matthews' whereabouts.
A large scale search party
was launched.
26th February, 2008

Relieved to hear Shannon Matthews has been found alive, a Dewsbury local tears up a 'missing girl' poster. The public had yet to learn Shannon's kidnappers were in fact her mother and her mother's partner.
14th March, 2008

Karen Matthews, mother of missing schoolgirl, Shannon Matthews, is taken from Dewsbury police station to appear before court for the abduction of her daughter. Karen Matthews and her partner, Michael Donovan, were later found guilty of kidnap, false imprisonment and perverting the course of justice. She was sentenced to eight years in jail.

9th April, 2008

Protesters clash with riot
police outside an annual
BNP Festival in Denby,
Derbyshire. 250 police
officers were deployed to
disperse the demonstration.
The day ended with 33
arrests.
16th August, 2008

Victims of violent crime and the families of those who had recently died in a spate of knife crime, march through London in a peace rally.
20th September, 2008

The Publishers gratefully acknowledge Press Association Images, from whose extensive archive the photographs in this book have been selected. Personal copies of the photographs in this book, and many others, may be ordered online at www.prints.paphotos.com

For more information, please contact:

Ammonite Press

AE Publications Ltd. 166 High Street, Lewes, East Sussex, BN7 1XU, United Kingdom
Tel: 01273 488005 Fax: 01273 402866
www.ammonitepress.com